STARS OF MYTHOLOGY

STARS OF INDIAN MYTHOLOGY

NANCY DICKMANN

Gareth Stevens PUBLISHING

Please visit our website, www.garethstevens.com. For a free color catalog of all our high-quality books, call toll free 1-800-542-2595 or fax 1-877-542-2596.

Cataloging-in-Publication Data
Names: Dickmann, Nancy. | Lilly, Matt, illustrator.
Title: Stars of Indian mythology / by Nancy Dickmann, illustrated by Matt Lilly.
Description: Buffalo, NY : Gareth Stevens Publishing, 2026. | Series: Stars of mythology | Includes glossary and index.
Identifiers: ISBN 9781482473339 (pbk.) | ISBN 9781482473346 (library bound) | ISBN 9781482473353 (ebook)
Subjects: LCSH: Mythology, Indic--Juvenile literature. | Hindu mythology--Juvenile literature.
Classification: LCC BL2001.3 D524 2026 | DDC 398.20954--dc23

Published in 2026 by
Gareth Stevens Publishing
2544 Clinton St.
Buffalo, NY 14224

First published in Great Britain in 2017 by The Watts Publishing Group

Credits
Series Editor: Sarah Peutrill
Consultant: Anita Ganeri
Series Design and Illustrations: Matt Lilly
Cover Designer: Cathryn Gilbert
Picture Researcher: Diana Morris

Pic credits: Viacheslav Belyaev/Dreamstime: 14c, 156c, 16bl, 17t, 17b, 18l, 20tl, 20cl. Bykelikova/Dreamstime: 6 bg. Jatin Chadra/ Dreamstime: 1cr, 22t, 25tl, 25bl, 25br. Cristaloid/Dreamstime: 1c, 18c, 20tc, 20tr, 20c, 20bl, 20bc, 21tl, 21c, 21cr, 21bl, 21br. David Evison/Dreamstime: 19c, 20br, 21tc, 21cl. http://www.freepik.com”>Designed by Freepik: front cover bg, 1 bg. Sean Higson/India Kolkata/Alamy: 10c, 12trc, 12bl, 13tl, 13bc. Jaret Kantepar/Shutterstock: front cover cl, 23c, 25bc, 32c. Claudine van Massenhove/Shutterstock: 4. Murali Nath/Dreamstime: front cover cr, 7, 8tl, 9bl, 10tc. Reddees/Shutterstock: 5. Jeremy Richards/Dreamstime: 26 bg. Shahril KHMD/Shutterstock: 23 bg. Singh Lens/Shutterstock: 25tr. Szefei/Shutterstock: 10-11 bg, 12t, 13t, 13b. Tantrik 71/Shutterstock: 29tc. Tinamou/Dreamstime: 14-15 bg. CC Wikimedia Commons: 1cl, 2cl, 2cr, 6c, 8tr, 9bc, 10tr, 11c, 12tl, 12tr, 12bc, 12br, 13tr, 13tc,13br, 26b, 27c, 28c, 28br, 29tl, 29tr.

Printed in the United States of America

CPSIA compliance information: Batch #CSGS26
For further information contact Gareth Stevens at 1-800-542-2595.

CONTENTS

HINDU MYTHOLOGY

Hinduism is one of the world's oldest religions. It began in India more than 3,000 years ago and is still practiced by millions of people today. Over the centuries, a complex mythology has developed. It involves a huge cast of characters, including gods, mortals, demons, and animals. The stories often have themes of good triumphing over evil, or they explain how things were created or destroyed.

GODS AND DEMONS

The Hindu stories are full of powerful beings. Two of the main types are gods (often called *devas*) and demons (called *asuras*). The gods and demons fight each other a lot. Like humans, they often marry and have children, but unlike humans, they have magical powers. Three of the gods were more important than the others: Brahma, the creator of life on earth; Vishnu, the protector of life; and Shiva, who destroys so that new things can be created.

HINDU TEMPLES SUCH AS THIS ONE IN INDIA ARE A PLACE WHERE PEOPLE CAN WORSHIP THE GODS.

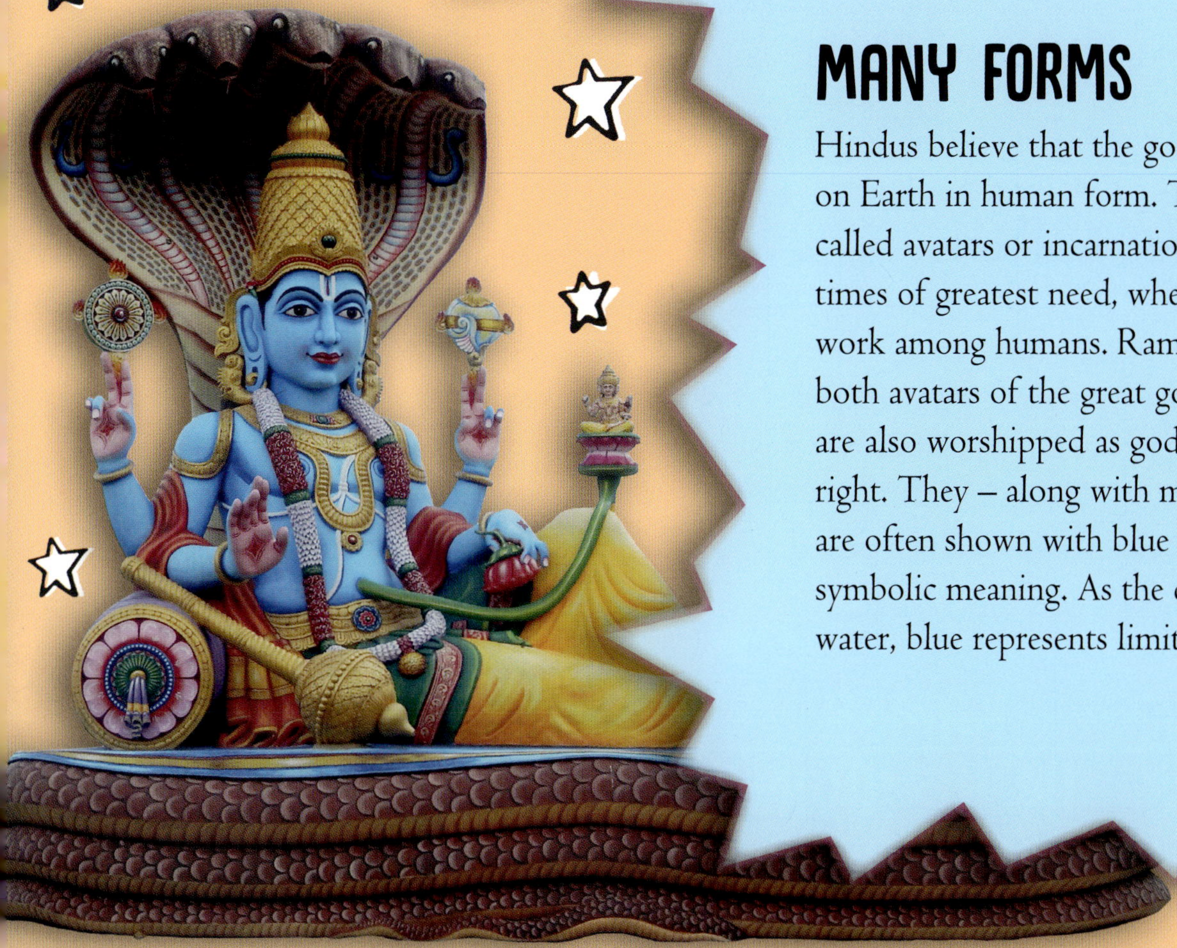

MANY FORMS

Hindus believe that the gods sometimes appear on Earth in human form. These forms are called avatars or incarnations. They appear at times of greatest need, when evil forces are at work among humans. Rama and Krishna are both avatars of the great god, Vishnu. They are also worshipped as gods in their own right. They – along with many other gods – are often shown with blue skin, which has a symbolic meaning. As the color of the sky and water, blue represents limitlessness.

SHOWING A GOD WITH MANY ARMS IS A WAY OF REPRESENTING HIS POWER OR HIS ABILITY TO DO MANY THINGS AT THE SAME TIME.

HOW DO WE KNOW?

For many years, the Hindu myths were passed down orally. They were later written down in the ancient language of Sanskrit. These writings include the *Vedas* – an early collection of hymns and prayers – and two long poems called the *Ramayana* and the *Mahabharata*, which recount the adventures of heroes and gods. These were sacred texts in the Hindu religion, and they still are today. Hindus still worship the gods, and they keep their sacred stories alive through dance and drama, just as they have done for thousands of years.

KAMSA AND KRISHNA

READ THEIR STORY ON PAGES 8–9.

Fact file: KAMSA

KAMSA was a cruel, greedy, and ruthless prince, and he overthrew his own father to take the throne. When he heard a prophecy that his sister Devaki's child would one day kill him, he threw Devaki and her husband into prison and killed each of their children as soon as it was born.

Over the years, Kamsa tried several times to kill Krishna. He sent demons and other beings to attack him, but Krishna always managed to kill them and escape. Kamsa knew that one day there would be a final showdown with Krishna.

KAMSA IN HIS OWN WORDS:

BROTHERLY LOVE:
So maybe it's not okay to throw your own sister in prison. But if her child is going to grow up to kill me, I'm taking no chances!

HOW TO STAY ON MY GOOD SIDE:
Tell me what a great king you think I am.

IT'S NOT EASY BEING EVIL:
I've done a lot of not-so-nice things to get where I am today. And I have a sneaking feeling that one day they may come back to bite me.

Fact file: KRISHNA

KRISHNA was the son of King Kamsa's sister Devaki and her husband, Vasudev. When Krishna was born, Vasudev managed to smuggle him out of the kingdom to save him from his wicked uncle. Krishna was raised by a cowherd, Nanda, and his wife, Yashoda.

As Krishna grew, Nanda taught him to be a cowherd. Krishna was known for his mischievous pranks, but also for his amazing deeds. There was a very good reason why Krishna wasn't an ordinary boy: he was one of the avatars of Vishnu.

KRISHNA IN HIS OWN WORDS:

FAMILY TIES:
I love my foster parents, but I wish I could see more of my real mother and father. One day I'll get them out of prison!

FAVORITE HOBBY:
Playing my flute. The girls love it!

WHY I'M SO BLUE:
Don't worry, it's not because I'm sad! Quite the reverse, in fact. But in pictures, I have blue skin to show my link to Vishnu.

BEST BUD:
My brother Balarama. We get up to all sorts of trouble together.

KRISHNA

WRESTLING FOR REVENGE

It was the most exciting contest in centuries: the king's champion wrestlers against the young challengers from across the river.

KING KAMSA

When the spectators gathered for this morning's wrestling contest, they were in no way prepared for the chaos that followed. King Kamsa's challenge had gone out through the countryside, bringing challengers from all over. A glittering prize awaited anyone who could beat his two giants, Chanura and Mushtika.

As the challengers started to arrive, all eyes were on Krishna and Balarama, two teenagers from a neighboring kingdom. Stories had been going around about Krishna's adventures fighting demons, but he didn't look big enough to pose much of a threat. His brother Balarama was built more like a wrestler, but even he was dwarfed by the king's giants.

It nearly began in disaster. As the boys arrived at the palace gate, a giant elephant broke loose from its chains and went on a rampage. "It was horrible," said an eyewitness. "The elephant was trumpeting like mad, trampling everything in its path." The crowds watched in amazement as Krishna raced up, threw the elephant to the ground, and killed it with one of its own tusks.

"From where I was standing, I had a good view of the royal box," said one onlooker. "And when Krishna killed that elephant, King Kamsa went white as a sheet."

Krishna had barely broken a sweat, and he now squared up to Chanura, while Balarama took on Mushtika. These two champions had gone undefeated for years, but now they had met their match. After a furious fight, both lay dead on the ground.

"The crowd was going wild, but I could tell that Krishna wasn't really listening," said one spectator. "He was looking over at the royal box. Before anyone knew what was happening, he had raced over, dragged the king out by his hair, and killed him!"

"My work here is done," said a triumphant Krishna, after the dust had settled. "I'm going to release my parents from prison and put the true king back on the throne. And then I'm going to celebrate!"

SAVITRI AND SATYAVAN

READ THEIR STORY ON PAGES 12–13.

Fact file: SAVITRI

Asvapati was the ruler of Madra kingdom, but he and his wife had been childless for many years. They prayed to the god Savitr and were eventually rewarded with the birth of a daughter, whom they named **SAVITRI** .

Savitri grew up to be so beautiful and pure that none of the men in the kingdom dared to ask for her hand in marriage. Her father then told her that she could choose her own husband, so she set off on a journey to find one.

SAVITRI IN HER OWN WORDS:

DADDY'S GIRL:
My father is the best. And I'm not just saying that because he lets me do what I want!

THE SIMPLE LIFE:
Who needs luxury? Satyavan showed me that you can live a simple life and still be happy.

TRIP OF A LIFETIME:
I went all over the country to look for a handsome prince to marry, before finding Satyavan. Who knew that a good man would be so hard to find?

SECRET FEAR:
Not much scares me - not even Yama, the god of death. But I'm terrified at the thought of having to live without Satyavan.

Fact file: SATYAVAN

SATYAVAN had spent most of his life in the forest, looking after his elderly parents, who were both blind. But although he was poor and lived a simple life, he was actually a prince. His father, Dyumatsena, had been ruler of Salwa kingdom until he was overthrown.

Savitri saw past Satyavan's shabby appearance and was impressed by his generosity and his loyalty to his parents. They fell in love and decided to marry.

SATYAVAN IN HIS OWN WORDS:

THOUGHTS ON ROYALTY:
It's hard to feel like a prince when you live in a tiny cottage with no servants.

MY FAMILY:
My father and mother didn't deserve to be blinded and forced into exile. They're good people, and it's my duty to look after them.

LOVE AT FIRST SIGHT:
I'd never seen anyone like Savitri. Even now that we're married, I still have to pinch myself sometimes to make sure that I'm not dreaming.

WHAT KEEPS ME AWAKE AT NIGHT:
I saw Savitri talking to a wise old prophet and looking worried. Did he make a prediction about my future?

LOVE CONQUERS ALL

... YAMA'S STORY

People always tell me that I'm too tender-hearted. And for the god of death, that's a real failing.

Take last week, when I went to collect the soul of a young man who had just died. I rode into the forest clearing and saw them: the beautiful young woman in tears as she cradled her husband's body.

I recognized them at once - their wedding, just a year ago, had caused quite a stir. Savitri was a princess, and no one could believe that her parents would let her marry a penniless woodcutter, even if he was actually a prince. There was also a rumor going around that a wise man made a prophecy that Satyavan would die within a year. But Savitri married him anyway. If that isn't love, what is?

But now he was dead, and she was a wreck. I felt bad, but I collected Satyavan's soul and started on my way. I hadn't gone far before I heard a noise and looked back. Savitri was following me. "What do you want?" I asked.

"I can't live without Satyavan," she pleaded. "Take me too."

"Don't be silly," I told her. I turned around and kept going. Every few minutes, though, I glanced back, and each time she was still there. You had to admire her persistence.

I stopped. "Oh, all right," I said. "I'll grant you a wish, as long as you don't ask for your husband's soul."

"Will you give Satyavan's parents back their sight?"

"Done." I continued on my way, but five minutes later ... you guessed it, she was still there. "Have another wish," I offered. "Same rules apply."

"Can Satyavan's father have his kingdom back?"

"Of course." But did that get rid of her? No. I was getting tired of it. "All right, have one more wish, but this is the last one."

Savitri's eyes gleamed. "May I be the mother of many sons?"

"Yes, fine! Now leave me alone!" But too late, I realized what I had done. Savitri couldn't become the mother of many sons - not without her husband. There was nothing else to do: I had to give his soul back.

See what I mean about being too soft-hearted?

RAMA AND SITA

READ THEIR STORY ON PAGES 16–17.

Fact file: RAMA

Like Krishna, **RAMA** was an avatar of Vishnu. His earthly parents were Dasharatha, the ruler of Ayodhya kingdom, and his wife Kaushalya. He had a happy childhood, growing up in the palace with his brothers.

Rama was known for being virtuous and dutiful. After marrying Sita, he voluntarily went into exile in the forest for 14 years, so that his father didn't have to break a promise that he had been tricked into giving.

RAMA IN HIS OWN WORDS:

MY POSSE:
My brother Lakshmana has stuck by me through thick and thin. And Hanuman the monkey keeps us all entertained.

LEAST FAVORITE RELATIVE:
My aunt Kaikeyi. I was supposed to inherit my father's throne, but her trickery got me exiled into the forest instead.

CLAIM TO FAME:
I'm stronger than anyone else I know.

COULDN'T LIVE WITHOUT:
My beautiful wife, Sita. She's the best thing that ever happened to me.

Fact file: SITA

SITA was a princess, the daughter of King Janaka and his wife Sunaina. But she was also an avatar of Lakshmi, the goddess of wealth and good fortune. Lakshmi was Vishnu's wife, so Sita was destined to marry Rama.

When Rama went into exile, Sita chose to go with him. During their time there, she was kidnapped by the demon king Ravana. As the perfect example of an ideal wife, she stayed faithful to Rama during her long imprisonment.

SITA IN HER OWN WORDS:

KEEPING IT IN THE FAMILY:
My younger sister Urmila fell in love with Rama's brother Lakshmana and married him. We are the queens of the double date!

HOME COMFORTS:
I would follow Rama anywhere, so of course I went into exile with him. But I do sometimes miss the little luxuries you get when you live in a palace.

MOST FAITHFUL FRIEND:
When Ravana kidnapped me, Jatayu the vulture king gave his life in order to tell Rama what had happened.

WEDDING OF THE YEAR

It's the royal wedding we've all been waiting for: tomorrow Rama and Sita tie the knot. In honor of the event, let's take a look back at how it all came about.

Some people thought that Sita might never get married. Her beauty, charm, and virtue meant that finding a man worthy of her was always going to be difficult. Her father, King Janaka, wanted only the best for his daughter, so once she came of age he decided to hold a contest.

"The king's plan was that suitors would come from far and wide," one of the palace servants told us. "He has this bow, you see – everyone says it once belonged to Lord Shiva. I don't know about that, but I can tell you that it was heavy. I was in charge of tidying the room where he kept it, and it was always getting in the way of my dusting. I couldn't move it an inch."

Anyone who wanted to marry Sita would have to lift and then string the bow. It seemed like an impossible task, and none of the princes who tried were able to do it.

"Then Rama walked in with his brother," one of Sita's ladies-in-waiting told us. "Ooh, he was lovely, and no mistake! Sita spotted him straightaway and asked who he was."

"She hadn't been paying much attention to the other princes," added another lady-in-waiting. "One by one, they all tried to lift the bow – you should have seen them strain and heave! But when it was Rama's turn, she sat up straight and didn't take her eyes off him."

Eyewitnesses said that Rama walked up to the bow and reached down to grasp it. Then he glanced up, caught Sita's eye and smiled. "It was like her gaze gave him strength," said the prince's brother, Lakshmana. "He lifted the bow without difficulty and strung it. In fact, he was so strong that he broke it!"

"Love at first sight, that's what it was," sighed the lady-in-waiting wistfully. "The minute they saw each other, they knew. It was just meant to be."

HANUMAN AND RAVANA

READ THEIR STORY ON PAGES 20–21.

Fact file: HANUMAN

HANUMAN was a monkey god with magical powers. He was one of Rama's most loyal helpers. Hanuman was incredibly strong and could also make himself bigger or smaller, and jump or fly huge distances. He was clever and mischievous, and annoyed other gods with his pranks.

Finally, the god Brahma decided that something had to be done. He cursed Hanuman so that he forgot about his magical powers. He could only use them again when someone reminded him about them.

HANUMAN IN HIS OWN WORDS:

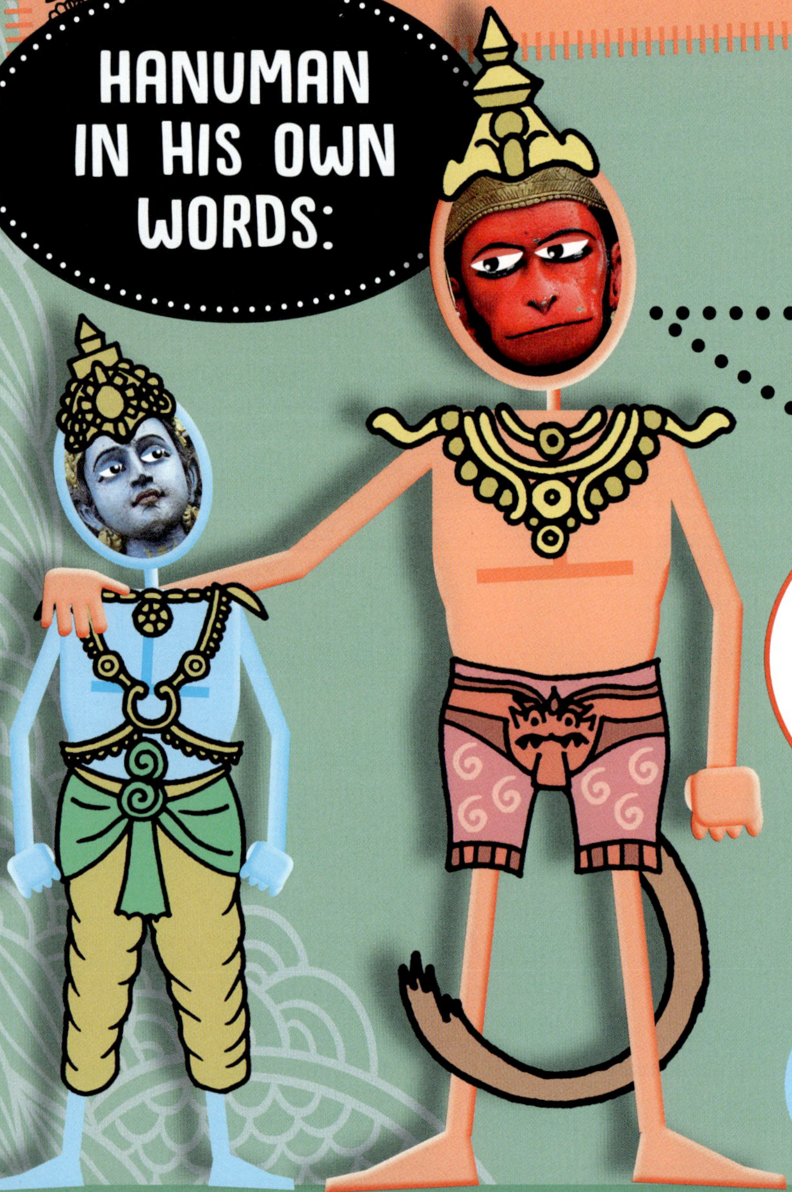

COME FLY WITH ME:
Some people say that my father is Vayu, the wind god. That would certainly explain why I'm able to fly!

SNACK TIME:
When I was young, I thought the sun was a ripe mango and tried to eat it. That did not go down well with Indra, the king of the gods. I can still feel it where his thunderbolt hit me!

FAVORITE HUMAN:
Rama's a great friend, and I'd do anything for him.

Fact file: RAVANA

RAVANA was an evil demon who ruled the kingdom of Lanka. He had ten heads and twenty arms, as well as magical powers. While Rama and Sita were living in exile in the forest, Ravana kidnapped Sita and flew with her back to his kingdom.

Ravana had once asked Brahma to grant him immortality, but the boon (special power) that Brahma granted only protected him from gods and demons. It was still possible for a human to kill him, and when Rama came to rescue Sita, he eventually killed Ravana.

RAVANA IN HIS OWN WORDS:

IT'S NOT EASY BEING ME:
With ten heads and 20 arms, the costs really mount up. Ten golden crowns, specially-made robes with 20 sleeves ... it's a wonder I'm not broke!

OUT FOR REVENGE:
Rama cut off my sister's nose, so I kidnapped his wife. Fair's fair, right?

WHY I DON'T LIKE MOUNTAINS:
Once I was trying to carry away Mount Kailash (bit of a long story) and Lord Shiva used his toe to press down the mountain and stop me. I was stuck under that mountain for a thousand years!

MONKEY MAYHEM

IF YOU SET SITA FREE, RAMA WILL SHOW MERCY. BUT IF YOU DON'T, HE WILL DESTROY YOU.
EXECUTE THIS CHEEKY MONKEY!
YOU CAN'T, MY LORD! HE'S ONLY A MESSENGER!
ALL RIGHT, JUST SET HIS TAIL ON FIRE INSTEAD.
HE'S GOING TO REGRET THAT!
But just as Hanuman's tail was set alight . . .
I'M FREE! NOW IT'S TIME TO CAUSE A BIT OF MAYHEM.
THIS IS FUN!
I THINK RAMA WOULD CONSIDER THAT A GOOD NIGHT'S WORK!
The end.

PARVATI AND GANESHA

READ THEIR STORY ON PAGES 24–25.

Fact file: PARVATI

PARVATI was one of the most important Hindu goddesses. Her father was Himavan, the lord of the mountains. Like many Hindu gods, Parvati could take different forms. She was usually kind and nurturing, but she could turn into the fierce Kali or the warrior Durga when needed.

After a long courtship, Parvati married the god Shiva. In many versions of the myths, Parvati is actually Shiva's first wife, Sati, reborn. She represented love, fertility, and devotion.

PARVATI IN HER OWN WORDS:

PATIENCE IS A VIRTUE:
I knew I wanted to marry Lord Shiva, but he took a lot of convincing. I spent years by his side before he finally took an interest.

HOME SWEET HOME:
Lord Shiva and I live at the top of Mount Kailash. The view from there is amazing!

FAVORITE COLOR:
Red. Don't you think I look good in it?

DON'T GET ME ANGRY:
I might just change into my warrior form, Durga, and do a bit of slaying.

Fact file: GANESHA

GANESHA, the son of Parvati and Shiva, is a popular Hindu god who is instantly recognizable because of his elephant's head. He is a god of beginnings, and people often worship him before starting any new project, to ensure success.

Ganesha is usually shown with a pot belly and is known for his appetite. He once was invited to a fancy banquet where he ate all the food, as well as the plates, decorations, and furniture! He also usually has a broken tusk. Some stories say that he broke off the tusk to use as a pen.

GANESHA IN HIS OWN WORDS:

CHECK OUT MY RIDE:

My favorite mount is a rat. If you want to know how an elephant can possibly ride a rat, all I can say is that I'm a god and can do whatever I want!

GUILTY PLEASURE:

You'll never find me without a handful of sweets.

SIBLING RIVALRY:

My brother Kartikeya still goes on about the time I beat him in a race to win the fruit of knowledge – he says I cheated!

TOP OF THE CLASS:

Got a question that needs answering? Try me – I'm the god of knowledge and wisdom.

HOW GANESHA GOT HIS HEAD

... PARVATI'S DIARY

What a weird day this has been! I created a child, lost him, then saw him brought back to life … all in a single day.

It all started when I decided to have a bath. Lord Shiva has an annoying habit of barging in on me when I'm in the tub. Usually I set someone to guard the door, but today I forgot. By the time I remembered, I couldn't be bothered to get out. So I rubbed some of the dirt off my body and formed it into the shape of a child, then breathed life into it.

I sent him to guard the door and watched him go with a smile on my face. He was an adorable little thing, cute and chubby. Perhaps, I thought, I could keep him as my own child. Lord Shiva is often away, and I get lonely.

The bath was lovely and warm, and I must have dozed off. The next thing I knew, there was an almighty commotion outside the door, and Lord Shiva burst in, carrying his sword. "What on earth is going on?" I asked him.

He scowled. "Some naughty child was standing outside the door and wouldn't let me come in."

It felt like the bottom had dropped out of my stomach. "Oh, dear," I gasped. "What have you done?"

"What have I done?" he repeated. "Chopped his head off, of course. That's what you get for disrespecting a god."

I was furious with him, and trust me, you don't want to see me when I'm angry. I took on the most fearsome form I could. "Listen, that boy was my son, and you're going to get him a new head and bring him back to life. Otherwise I will destroy all of creation!"

Lord Shiva gulped. "What kind of head?" he asked.

"I don't care! The first one you find!"

So off he went, and before long he came back … with an elephant's head. I sighed as he placed it on poor Ganesha's body, bringing him back to life.

So my lovely boy now has a trunk. Better than nothing, I guess!

HIRANYAKASHIPU AND PRAHLADA

READ THEIR STORY ON PAGES 28–29.

Fact file: HIRANYAKASHIPU

HIRANYAKASHIPU was a demon king who ruled over a race of giants. He hated Vishnu because his younger brother had been killed by Varaha, one of Vishnu's avatars. Hiranyakashipu became obsessed with gaining magical powers so that he could get his revenge.

As part of his plan, Hiranyakashipu spent years in fasting and penance, hoping to please Brahma. Finally, Brahma granted him a boon (a special power). He didn't quite promise immortality, but it was good enough for Hiranyakashipu.

HIRANYAKASHIPU IN HIS OWN WORDS:

WHO'S NUMBER ONE?
I'm strong, I'm powerful, and I'm indestructible. I can't see why anyone would bother worshipping anyone else but me.

STICKS AND STONES MAY BREAK MY BONES ...
But do you know what will never hurt me? No man, beast, or weapon can ever kill me, thanks to my friend, Lord Brahma.

BIGGEST DISAPPOINTMENT:
My own son won't stop going on about his hero. Lord Vishnu this, Lord Vishnu that, all day long. He needs to put a sock in it!

Fact file: PRAHLADA

PRAHLADA was Hiranyakashipu's son. While his mother was pregnant with him, she lived for a while under the protection of the wise man Narada. His teachings had an effect, even on her unborn child. As Prahlada grew, he became a devoted follower of Vishnu.

Hiranyakashipu was furious that his own son was so devoted to his sworn enemy. He eventually decided to kill Prahlada and made several attempts. But no matter what he tried, Prahlada remained loyal to Vishnu. In return for this loyalty, Vishnu made sure that Prahlada was never harmed.

PRAHLADA IN HIS OWN WORDS:

MY PARENTS:
My mother's great, but my father is another story. He's convinced that he's the greatest being in the universe, when everyone knows that he's nothing compared to Lord Vishnu.

A WAY WITH ANIMALS:
My father once tried to have me trampled by elephants, but they didn't hurt me. When he locked me in a room full of venomous snakes, that didn't work either.

IS IT JUST ME, OR IS IT WARM IN HERE?
My aunt Holika couldn't be harmed by fire, so my father ordered her to carry me onto a burning pyre. Guess what? Even that didn't work!

NOT SO IMMORTAL AFTER ALL

Ding, dong, the king is dead - even though he was supposed to be immortal! In this exclusive interview, his son Prahlada explains how it all went down.

INTERVIEWER:
Let's start by saying how sorry we all are to hear of the loss of your father, Hiranyakashipu.

PRAHLADA:
Sorry? Don't be! Do you know how many times he's tried to kill me?

INTERVIEWER:
Speaking of killing, wasn't it supposed to be impossible to kill Hiranyakashipu?

PRAHLADA:
Sort of. The exact wording of Lord Brahma's boon said that he couldn't be killed at night or during the day; by man or beast; by any weapon; or inside or outside.

INTERVIEWER:
That sounds pretty comprehensive.

PRAHLADA:
Well, my father certainly thought so! That's what made him bold enough to try to kill me – his own son and a devotee of Lord Vishnu. But he was so convinced that his boon from Lord Brahma made him indestructible, he never realized that my love for Lord Vishnu does the same for me.

INTERVIEWER:
And this was put to the test?

PRAHLADA:
Yesterday we were arguing and I told him that Lord Vishnu was everywhere - in fire, in water, even in this crumbling old pillar in the courtyard. So he tied me to the pillar and raised his sword, to prove that Lord Vishnu couldn't save me.

INTERVIEWER:
What happened next?

PRAHLADA:
It was amazing! Lord Vishnu burst out of the pillar, but he was in the form of his avatar Narasimha - half man, half lion. Do you see? He was neither man nor beast!

INTERVIEWER:
Yes, but what about the other protections of Lord Brahma's boon?

PRAHLADA:
It was dusk when this all happened - neither night nor day, but something in between. And then Narasimha dragged him to the doorway of the palace, so he was neither inside nor outside.

INTERVIEWER:
Very clever! How did he get around the thing about no weapon ever killing your father?

PRAHLADA:
He didn't need a weapon; he used his sharp lion's claws to tear Hiranyakashipu apart. Lord Vishnu proved how powerful he is.

INTERVIEWER:
So now you're the king?

PRAHLADA:
And I promise to be a kinder one than my father was!

GLOSSARY

AVATAR a human incarnation of a god

BOON something that is a help or benefit. Gods often granted boons to mortals and other beings, such as immortality or protection from fire.

CURSE to say magical words that will cause trouble or bad luck for something

DEMON an evil spirit or being that often causes harm or destruction

DEVOTEE a strong believer in a particular religion or god

EXILE a situation in which a person is forced to leave their home and go live somewhere else

FASTING eating very little food - or none at all - in order to receive a spiritual benefit

FERTILITY the ability to have babies

IMMORTALITY the ability to live forever and never die or decay. The Hindu gods and goddesses were immortal.

INCARNATION a person on Earth who is a form of a god

INHERIT to receive something (such as money or a title) from someone else when they die

MORTAL an ordinary person who will eventually die instead of living forever

MYTH a traditional story that tries to explain why the world is the way that it is, or to recount legendary events

ORALLY by mouth. Here it refers to how myths are told as stories, passed down the generations through storytelling.

OVERTHROW to remove a king or other ruler from power, often by force

PENANCE actions that you do in order to show how sorry you are for having done something wrong

PROPHECY a prediction about something that will happen in the future

PROPHET a person who can predict what will happen in the future

PYRE a large pile of wood or other fuel that is set on fire

REINCARNATION the idea that after death, a person's soul can be reborn into a different body

SOUL the spiritual part of a person, which can't be seen or touched like their human body can

SUITOR a man who wants to marry a particular woman

THUNDERBOLT an imaginary pointed missile that flies down to earth along with a lightning flash

VIRTUE behavior showing high moral standards

BOOKS

We are Hindus (My Religion and Me),
Philip Blake, Franklin Watts

Hinduism (Religion in Focus), Geoff Teece, Franklin Watts

Seasons of Splendour: Tales, Myths and Legends of India,
Madhur Jaffrey, Puffin Books

Stories from India, Anna Milbourne, Usborne

WEBSITES

This website has general information about the Hindu religion:
https://www.bbc.co.uk/bitesize/articles/zmpp92p

Here you'll find information on many of the main Hindu gods and goddesses:
http://www.sanatansociety.org/hindu_gods_and_goddesses.htm

Go here to read dozens of stories from Hindu mythology:
http://www.kidsgen.com/fables_and_fairytales/indian_mythology_stories/

Note to parents and teachers: Every effort has been made by the Publishers to ensure that these websites are suitable for children, that they are of the highest educational value, and that they contain no inappropriate or offensive material. However, because of the nature of the internet, it is impossible to guarantee that the contents of these sites will not be altered. We strongly advise that internet access is supervised by a responsible adult.

INDEX